DENIZENS

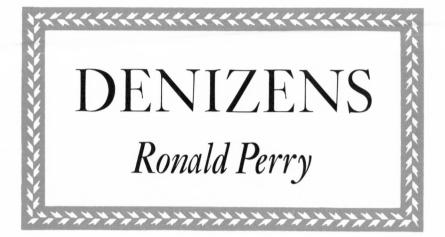

DENIZENS

Ronald Perry

RANDOM HOUSE   NEW YORK

Versions of some of the poems in this book were originally published in
magazines, and acknowledgment is gratefully made to the editors of the following
for permission to reprint them here:

Charlatan. "The Dreamtakers" (under the title "The Anniversary").

Epoch. "Pavane in the Form of an Elegy"; "Testament"; Sections I, IV, and
VI of "Nightsongs & Laments" (under the titles "Written in a Park in Autumn,"
"Song at Summer's End," and "Point Charles"); Sections II and III of "Three
Birds" (under the titles "The Phoenix" and "The Hawk"); "The Centaur"; and
"Epilogue for a Bestiary."

The Hudson Review. Section II of "Nightsongs & Laments" (under the title
"Nocturne"); Sections I–IX of "After the Lao" (under the titles "Nightsong:
Thamnāret," "Two Invocations," "The Song of Sétaphon," "The Song of
Mahāxay," "The Song of Nhômphibàne," "The Call of the Soul," and "Invocation:
Soukhouan"); Section II of the poem titled "Two Poems after the Indonesian of
Chairil Anwar" (under the title "Voices"); and "Scrollpainting."

Poetry. "Suite for Wind Instruments"; Sections V and VII of "Nightsongs &
Laments" (under the titles "Pigeon Key" and "Le Quattro Stagioni III"); and "Aria
& Variations."

Quarterly Review of Literature. "In Lieu of Many Ornaments" (under the
title "Epithalamion"); "For James, on His Birthday"; Section I of "Four Poems
from the Hungarian Revolution" (under the title "History Lesson"); "Tiger-Balm
Gardens"; and Section I of "Three Birds" (under the title "The Peacock").

Spectrum. "The Bonepickers."

The Western Review. Section III of "Nightsongs & Laments" (under the title
"Elegy for Blue Piano").

Sections II, III and IV of "Four Poems from the Hungarian Revolution,"
(under the titles "As Witness to Your Suffering," "Anniversary: October 23, 1963,"
and "Testament") are reprinted from David Ray: *From the Hungarian Revolution.*
Copyright © 1966 by Cornell University. Used by permission of the publisher,
Cornell University Press. Two of them, I and III, were subsequently included in
Gloria Victris, edited by Tibor Tollas (Nemzetör, Munich, 1966).

A musical setting of "Nightsongs & Laments VI," by Anthony Strilko, was published by Mercury Music Publishers (New York, 1960), under the title "Point Charles."

Library of Congress Cataloging in Publication Data
Perry, Ronald, 1932–
Denizens.
(National poetry series)
I. Title. II. Series.
PS3531.E7193D4   811'.5'4   79–5531
ISBN 0–394–50962–5
ISBN 0–394–73856–X pbk.

Manufactured in the United States of America
24689753
First Edition

All of these
Of course
Are for John

"Near the exit, my flares burn out, and
I am left in darkness . . ."

"We divers have an expression: 'You pay for
your trip on the way out.'"

—Jacques Cousteau, *Blue Holes*

The National Poetry Series was established in 1978 to publish five col-
lections of poetry annually through five participating publishers. The
manuscripts are selected by five poets of national reputation. Publica-
tion is funded by James A. Michener, Edward J. Piszek, The Ford
Foundation, The Witter Bynner Foundation, and the five publishers—
Doubleday, E. P. Dutton, Harper & Row, Random House, and Holt,
Rinehart & Winston.

The National Poetry Series, 1980

Sterling A. Brown, *Collected Poems* (Selected by Michael Harper)
Joseph Langland, *Any Body's Song* (Selected by Ann Stanford)
Ronald Perry, *Denizens* (Selected by Donald Justice)
Wendy Salinger, *Folly River* (Selected by Donald Hall)
Roberta Spear, *Silks* (Selected by Philip Levine)

CONTENTS

ONE

SOME PAPER FLOWERS

for W.M. and J.H.

I'm sitting here looking
At your paper flowers
Wondering if you brought them
All the way from Mexico
As we did—eight, ten, eleven—
Who knows how many years ago?

They look the same. The dust
They wear as lightly as pollen
Tastes as ours did. One
Could swear they were not
Merely alike, but identical.

Of course it is not
Possible. You never had a chance
To see, much less acquire,
Our paper flowers
From the yellow bees hovering
About the trashcan to which,
Reluctantly, we finally consigned them.

And yet, slightly disheveled, wearing
Their delicate dry coats
Of dust, these withering flowers
Still retain exactly the same

Russet, wild strawberry, hay-
Fevered summer apricot
And cut-grass colors. I want
To touch them. I want to
But cannot. Too many years
Of ambush lie between.

3

"IN LIEU OF MANY ORNAMENTS"

for M.W.

Go, go to your marriage, be kind,
Landlord. Tell her for me,
These words are for the wind,
And for the wind only.
As, autumns, evenings, in the mind
Words darken, turn autumnal, fall
Through falling worlds of trees,
Fall towards yourself, and gardener be,
Or that daft bird your hands
Cage; but be beautiful, be kind.

Tell her, these footfalls in the leaves
Are wind's—not hers, not yours,
But a fitful music that deceives
Even itself, that doors
Are closed to, madman grieves
By, she must dance to, all
This fall, under the falling trees.
In this quick weather, safe indoors,
Tell her, the wind, with bloody hands,
Is tugging at the leaves.

FOR JAMES, ON HIS BIRTHDAY

In return, these few lessons in an old
And lovely drug, as long and various
As there are worlds farther than genius,
Worked out in subtlest algebras and told
To children in a kind of school for gold.
To learn light at one's fingertips, and thus
Learn love: by loss, all that's ambiguous,
Original, is so much more than gold.

It's what's behind it, and the statue's eyes:
At heart of light, the sun's stone disciplines;
What saint saw in his "painted paradise"
Extended, written in the ink of friends,
Until all that scribbling madmen can devise
Is only farther worlds for your surprise.

PAVANE IN THE
FORM OF AN ELEGY

after Ravel

How can I make an elegy
For her when she is not dead
Until tomorrow in the nursery-
Rhyme she cowered and read
As a child in a blue window?
How can I speak for the dead
Who walk through the low
Gardens on crutches, weaving
In her crooked dreams like snow
Falling, like leaves, grieving,
Beside themselves at the death
She did them to, believing
The world was nothing less
Than a vision in her cramp?
How can I write her death
Into the wind when the hump-
Backed cripple knows his fix,
And tramples her under his stump?

Her eyes are clawed by a fox-
Eyed prince; her heart
Is ripped by a gardener's picks;
The roses twist and start
At her step; a witch's oven
Blooms at her heart.

Because as a child she was given
The dark as a gift outright,
She locks herself now in a prison
Of birds, shutters the light

With an intricate window
That slices the terrible night
Into stars, insects, snow-
Creatures whirling under
Her feet. She will grow
Down to a knowledge of wonder,
Deeper than she is buried,
As the moon rides under
The street. She will be married
To her fox-eyed prince,
Truer than she is buried,
In the ghost of a dance.

Her eyes will find the shape
Of a leaf; her hands
Will tug at the roots that snap;
Under the house, the surgery
Of stems will cut her shape.

TESTAMENT

I pray you take these books
And give them to a fool
Nor get in return
Any that can be loved
Like these, as I was loved
Once before a death
For none whom death has moved
Nor any but a fool
Can but burn and be
Burned, as these books burn;

That I did once love well
All those who rode asleep
And sad on my white wall
The Lady in twelve tones
Of gold and brown give
(Because she is all light
Deep down to her bones)
Back to herself and tell
Her she is all light
Because she is loved well;

And such as now are left
Of letters do you return
(After this silence)
Upon your own sweet death
To those whom once they loved
And lost in the deft
Night, under the sides
Of stones, as your, as my own
Words turn back to stone
After this, in the stone ground.

SUITE FOR WIND INSTRUMENTS

for R.G.

From this island, the sea is always visible.
Every town has its view locked in fathoms.
Every eminence is a gull's promontory.

The sound of wings and the wind's sound
Are indistinguishable: one winged and windy sound
For a dark town in a drowned land.

Sun's color suits a man. Oleander.
Regiments of children forgive the park
Its lost colognes, its assignations.

Knee-deep in flowers. Cinq heures de l'après-midi.
The loving hour. Six. Roots nibble slyly
At my feet. Sept. The moon tugs at my shadow.

Who is she, the woman walking at evening
Into the amazement of her own image,
Reflected, among vines, in the jungle pool?

In my house of vines are many countries.
When I walk in the north, through the valleys of fires,
I walk alone. My father is in January.

Snapshot: boy flying his heart like a kite,
Like a silver fish, like a stringed instrument
Singing an old song that will be forgotten.

On any street, in any breathless evening,
I will have six bronze birds inside my drum
To court the jungle of your astonishment.

Mountains, like falling leaves, clatter
In the heartland. Bigger than these,
My heart falls like a stone towards the sea.

Aux Cayes! Southward, windward, return
To the sea. In the original spring,
All the world was green, like this green.

THE DREAMTAKERS

Another year is dead, and yet
We live, as still another sun
Comes tumbling down, alive, undone,
And down another moon, to drown
Each midnight with its dazed perfumes
And make unsteady every ground
On which we've stood.

                       But we forget—
For how shall we remember now,
Who sit in circles, shuttered rooms,
Outside the circle of the moon,
What once this sun was wont to sing?
And who of us remember how,
One day in such another spring,
Another sun, another moon
Came down, alive, like these, too soon?

THE GUILT OF THE GOLD FLOWER

I'd rather be someone, anyone
Else: weak-kneed
Or tall or mustached or bald or
Beautiful: anyone
With the capacity to become
Someone else: a man
With the world
Still whole and ripening in his fist:
A boy with a lisp
And brand-new eyes: a total
Wreck: all hands
Lost: a gold-
Bearing, glittering derelict.

A BIRTHDAY

for S.B.

Birthdays are for the lucky,
For the lovely, he said.
There are few
Competent enough to be glad.
To be sad,
Bad and indifferent
Is what most of us have.

But is that all, he said,
That can be hoped for, all
That we can ask
Of Grandpa, giggling Grandma: cards
From a crippled Uncle
Or maybe, on this unlucky
Wednesday, a note from Dad?

Whatever happens, in whatever
Way, he said, it is never
Wholly, exactly
What one expected. There will be
Other birthdays, attended,
Celebrated by others,
Other times and places

Unforeseen, unannounced, alone—
Until, on a time, will also come
The last one,
Without Grandpa, Uncle or Dad.
What will you do then?
Birthdays are for the lucky,
For the lovely, he said.

Few would choose to walk
 Alone, untried, unfamiliar,
In this imperfect
 Approximation of desolation.
Here, where the dwarf
 Orchids, said to be native,
Flourish only by taking
 The same hue, the same
Trouble to bloom and be born
 As the dwarf trees they hide in;
Here, where there is
 Little of the lush south
Straddling the green tropic,
 Much less of the apple-
Cheeked north, with its bluebirds
 And shorn pale lawns,
Its careful summer gardens
 Nuzzling conifer or pine—
Surely even the rarest,
 Happiest, most original
Imagination cannot construe
 A simple
Cross-country stroll,
 Alone, unaccompanied, but invited?
Nonetheless, a fact.
 There are those for whom
Even these sunburnt, shabby acres
 Are more promising, perhaps,
Than home. (Sometimes,
 Though not, of course,
Always.) Here, for example
 (Admittedly with a dog

Safely at heel), someone
        Is presently walking. After all,
He says, mostly to himself
        (But not only), the fire ants
Are not always deadly, all leaves
        Are not always
Poison oak or ivy. One finds
        One does not invariably need
The solace of birdsong.
        Take the palms. If they're not
Really palms, they're
        Certainly palmettos. And
Here, my friend,
        You'll find, I think, as I did,
That no one
        Need dig too deep
For bones, or limestone.

After swimming each night for years
In a pool of colored light
You stood still at the exact
Center of the stage, drowned
In applause. You were wearing silk
And silver, and your wings shook
At the least touch
Of wind.

        Then, without a word
To anyone, you ran away
To the coldest islands in the world
And took up gardening. But
One by one the flowers
Died. Each poem
Was another suicide. Nothing
Was left but your own voice
And the wrong voice of the rain.

And so you ran again:
Down to the sea and took ship
And didn't even try
To protest when forced
To make love to a few men
And war on the rest.

        And then you ran
And ran again: all the long way
Home. But
All the locks on all the doors
Were rusted fast. Falling

Roses choked the drive, and the nailed
Walls bled.

        And so, in this way,
For years you ran, hands
Over ears, heart over heels, down
To the very bottom of the world,
And then the whole way back again,
To a floating piece of the world
At the wrong end of summer.

                Here,
The flowers, though strange, yet
Live. But you have learned
To run too well,
And must again before the end—
Which will not come
Until you stand still at the exact
Center of your life,
And finally break into bloom,
Unlike your flowers or your poems.

TWO

NIGHTSONGS & LAMENTS

I

If I cover your mouth
With leaves,
If I plant you standing
In six feet of warm sand,
If I fill your hands
With pinecones
And start a flowering vine
Climbing to your eyes,
Will you talk to the wind
Like the casuarinas
And tell me who I am?

At sunfall, behind screens,
Looking out, the trees
Are ghosts of table-legs,
And the improbability of dusk's
A perpetual surprise.

Sunfall in a Mexican dish,
Yellow and red.
The repetition of similar
Sea and sky
In a world of cabinets.

Now the chairs have eyes
In their rungs, and sorrow
Is an imperfection,
An insistence on grief
That implies permanence.

Sunfall. The arrangement
Of faces on a magazine cover,
Complacent, inviolable:
Apple turned orange
In the detail of the wax fruit.

III

Now there are horns in the ceiling,
And rain stutters blankly on the keys.
The candle flickers down the room:
Points of light, branching trees.

The trombones underneath the eaves
Reiterate their muted epitaphs:
The blankest blue, the blue of brass,
The trombones whining in the eaves.

These are not my fingers on the keys
That pick the fitful strings of violins
And mutter blankly on the drums.
The horns are hidden in the leaves.

IV

for J.M.

Touch me, my love, in the dark and know
(Though what we know is better left unsaid)
These voices from a stone that come and go.

It is not meet that, loving, we should show
Aught of what we got by heart or head.
So touch me, love, in the dark and know

Stars, stones—their music only. Although
The moon has dropped and all the birds have fled,
These voices from a stone still come and go.

Perhaps we fashion better than we know,
Here, in this dark, on this dark bed.
Only touch me, love, and the dark will glow

With rivers of stars whose constellations flow
In giant landscapes drowsy with the dead.
Their voices from a stone will come and go,

And tell us nothing of that world below,
But of another, wilder world instead.
Touch me, my love, in the dark and know
These voices from a stone that come and go.

V

At moonrise, when the tide withdraws,
The world dissolves to a white yard.
Gestures of the grazing moon

Surround the heart, and all the hidden
Voices of the black bay
Speak in tongues that no one can remember:

Psalms of egrets, litany of gulls,
Parabolas and circles to the sky.
This is world of your dimension,

Old man sewn close in your nets.
Wake now, and walk
In these processions of the dead.

Hi lo— lo,
The spoonbill
Whose wings are yellow:
Bluegum is sorrow,
And the plums
Are the color of smoke.

Dogfennel and firefall.
And children rise
Like turtles from their eggs
On the sand, to my hand
The fostering
Of their shellback
Humped color.

In the mangrove-stand,
Where the spoonbill feeds
At the wrinkled,
Astonished heart:
Hi lo— lo,
Bluegum is sorrow.

VII

Summer's over
Skies are falling
Birds are flying
Farther on.
Sun's a diver
Always sailing
Down to dying
Like a stone.

August's into
Dry September
Thunder threatens
From the south.
All that we know
Or remember
Is forgotten
Like a death.

Like desire
This year's failing
Birds are burning
Burning air.
Trees on fire
Leaves are falling
Lovers turning
Foreign where

Once familiar
Islands glided
Gardens floated
In green air.
Upside down, we're
Still persuaded
And defeated
Everywhere.

THREE

ARIA & VARIATIONS

I

Once, I hungered for the tall
Timber of architecture:
To nail the cross-beams and hang
The whole house in empty air:
With a stone-adze or a hammer
Stamp steel, slice stones:
Where before there had been
Nothing, toss up
Tensions, towers, light's multiple
Refractions: to raise
Clean columns to the groins
Of the arches: the immaculate Nude
And the white porches. Later, I wanted
Black iron and marble: baroque
Comment: the sun's
Wires, stigmata, screens:
To put away
Beginning: to see the end
And the last roof
Lifted. Now, as I climb
The elegant, impossible stairway,
I feel I would like
To be like the interior:
Finished, polished, blinding.

Canon in contrary motion:
I am now more than myself
Diminished. I am alone.
I am crest and heart
Fallen.

Simple fugue! I
Waltz, a kind of country fool,
A bumpkin—until the oboe
And the flute turn
And return, and the subject
Is once more inverted.

Then am I
Doubled, adrift, among:
Only another
Distant, dissolving point of light
Woven of the silence.

Unfinished: woven
Of that which falls between
Two notes,
Two perfect, matching stones.

III

But inside, always, the gold
Ground, and the foursquare, air-
Shaped house
Of illusion. A window on the world,
Or the world's own window?
Opens in or opens out? As long
As there is open
Sky at the ends of the fingers
It does not matter. As long
As there is the briefest, northern
Touch of light, there will be
The blue potential. As
Long as you live in your own
Heart's house, from which the loving
Eye, gone blind, guides the green
Thumb, wrist and elbow,
It will be well, it must be well—
Moonlight, midnights: as the deft
Brush flies upward, and the lover's
Open eye discloses
That whole army of lovers
In the arms of their gardens:
As wrist pivots, in half-light,
Over the hidden
Landscapes under the carved
Faces, and the open palm gives up
The rarest jade, the least vermilion.

IV

Sometimes, too, I still
Walk around in the world's
Envelope. The blue air
Surrounds me. The clouds
Drown me. The trees,
For all their distant, faultless green,
Are inside, as I am.

As, at twilight, the gold
Pours up from the tall
Taproot, and you have only
To catch it in your cupped palms
To make a poem.

Then, you will have
The whole air. You will have
The light
At the ends of your fingers. You
Will have
What you came for.

FOUR

MAPS

Hell has been described.
I have also seen it dissembled.
Cartographers still dote on it.
The gilded manuscripts! The maps!
Sometimes, it's the interior
Of a volcano, with individual
Bonfires describing, articulating
Every sinew, nerve and bone. Other-
Wise and times it's cold:
Wolves too long in the tooth,
Gone strangely tame,
With fading, scarlet tongues,
Suddenly find themselves
Locked in crystal.
                Meanwhile,
Crabbed in tiny letters anywhere
In a margin, an especially
Blank piece of sky, heaven
Happens—as, perhaps,
In the middle of a desert, rock-
Salt towers out of green palms
Shiver, shatter
Mirage after mirage—
Then bury the imagined lake
Somebody real has drowned in.

STONECRAFT

Let the eye go first, then follow it
Into the stone: into
Granite, limestone or marble:
Behind the blind façade
Of pyramid or cathedral:
Between the walls
Of temples, toppled towers,
Palaces and buried houses. And then,
If you do not stop, if you do not stop
Too soon, the hand will also learn,
And carry of its own accord
Towards the broken
Column's sunlit interior
And the statue's heart
Locked in dry rock. Go on. Go
Deeper: into any
Grave, grind or hailstone:
Where even the wrists of vines
Cannot force entry
Nor the slow moss nor the ivy
Extend their knowledge of ruin. And then,
If you do not stop, if you do not stop
Too soon, the stone will take you
As it takes the light: beyond
Basalt, brimstone or jewel:
Under the pages of hieroglyphics
And the classic friezes:
Past the inscriptions, death-
Notices, runes, as you
Follow where eye and hand must go
And cannot stop until you stand
At the end on the other side,
Utterly alone.

FOUR POEMS FROM THE HUNGARIAN REVOLUTION

I
HISTORY LESSON

Buda, 1956. October
Rising, and the risen moon
Huger and redder than harvest
Over the rifled orchards, the floating
Fields and the pale
Faces, the fine
Bones of the skulls already showing,
The ruined hands suddenly
Opening like flowers: "Death,
Get drunk by yourself, we will escape . . ."

Long before the eagles
Fell to the Germans and the last
Emperor rolled
Naked on the tangled furs
With the stinking Northern
Shepherd boys and the white snow leopards
Walked beneath the broken lintels
A thousand times
And a thousand times they said
"There has been nothing quite like
This riot of ruin."

　　　　　Now tanks
Trample the red poppies
In the same fields where once,
The night before another battle,
The soft white footfall of padding

Moon-cat left the lucid
Prints of its claws for all to see
On half a legion's foreheads.

So too these self-
Same fields that once grew
Fatter on the blood of eagles
Will drink this iron rain also,
And push up in no time
The same sweet grass
As leafed in shield and helmet,
Blossomed in the empty cuirass.

II
THE CONFESSION
after the Hungarian of Vince Sulyok

When still, not two months ago,
We shared a room and a cobweb
With three hundred others; where each night
The rats came also, and each day
Tangled in your beard we stumbled
From one barbed wire to another
Between the club-faced man
And the man with the bludgeon;
When, during the lost days
And the last desperate nights
In the sewer, somehow we learned
That dark was not the only color,
Nor bitter the only taste of despair—
(Remember how close you sat beside me
That night we drove through October
By way of Miskolc and Eger,
With the lighted eyes of the tanks
Continually on us, and the guns
Stacked under the seat? or how
When we ran you couldn't tell
Your shoulder from my shoulder?)—
You were so ready to die you forgot
What it was like to be alive.

Now, there are seas between us,
Swamp, river and mountain.
Now, after only two months,
I cannot quite seem to remember
What it was like to rest
My head on your cold shoulder.

41

Now, each night when I'm clean
I go for a walk, wearing
A white shirt, between tall
Houses and gardens, all the way
From Oslo down to the beach
To listen to the ships.
Their sails are full of wind,
And on the road by the quay
Blond girls turn and look at me.
Here, where the elegant long cars
Race the light as it falls
Towards summer and the clean sea,

Suddenly I collapse on an empty
Crate and the barbed wire sprouts
Like a vine in my throat as I
Remember and once more take up
The coward's curse—who ran
Screaming when the tanks finally came
And hid under the very stones
Of the wall they stood you up against.

You, dead in Kistarcsa, dead
In Budapest and Recsk,
Although the only battle-flags
I can ever hoist now are these
Indifferent words spelling
Your names from the nameless
Graves wherein you lie—
Forgive me, if you can,
Because I turned and fled.

III
INTERPOLATION & COMMENT
ON A POEM BY GÁBOR KOCSIS

If you go at all, you must
Step lightly. Quicklime
Underfoot is still
Feeding, under the hollow street. At
The first wrong step
Another column's
Toppled and the bone-dry bricks
Collapse to let you stumble
Headlong, as before,
Into the shadow's mouth. Oh yes

There will be new walls
Out of the latest
Season's rubble, new glass
For the sagging window-frame. But
The eyes of the back-
Broken houses
Are still looking your way. Admit

That everywhere the world
Is dying. Here, it may even be
That the last shadow has already
Finally fallen. And yet,

One cannot help knowing
It is, even now, even here, more like
The shadow of a held
Hand, than the actual shape
Of the dark.

LETTER FROM PRISON
after the Hungarian of "B"

If I should die, friends,
Mention it—
So that at least I can continue
Living a little longer
In your poems—
As, even now, among
Anyone's old words on discolored
Love letters still lingers
The pale scent
Of somebody's great-grandmother's pressed
Flower.

I have no sons,
But if I am not permitted
To carve my own
Face with my own two hands,
Your few words
At least will keep me
Almost alive a little while longer.

A HOSPITAL POEM
FOR MY MOTHER

It's all too much. The deck's
Overloaded. The wheel
Won't stop turning. It's a fix. The dice
Are nineteen-
Sided.
          Okay and
Alas, my dear. It's all
Too true. If it's the truth
We're looking for
(And what else is worth the gamble?)
We've got it. The question now
Is, as always, what
To do with it?
              If the crooked
Dealer's almost unintelligible mumble
Makes any sense at all
It is, "Nothing. Do
Nothing. Wait. Be
What you have always been. Be
And accept."

FOR FATHER PUGH

The things we talk about most,
Money and worry,
We share
With almost everybody: how much

And how hard the cash is
In hand or in
The bank; how many and what kind
Of pills, bottles, heart's

Reluctant needles
This one requires, that one
Denies; what should, or can, be said
To Sarah or Mary, poor Amy

Whose husband's dying
Of some peculiar but dazzling
Poem unfolding
Like a map in his head: how long

Must we stay here, visiting
The spruce asylum of
This one's conversation, the unnecessary
Jail of that one's conversion?

A GIFT, PERHAPS, IN THE MAKING

for Maggie

I wish I had something better than this
To give you. A box of broken
Black chocolates, an occasional summer
Carefully bottled in green glass,

The odd rose petal or leaf
Candied and pressed
Between the clean pages just short of
The heart of a book. These are not,

I agree, nearly enough. If only
Words were less deadly
I might wish
I could find something more than this

To persuade or dissuade you. I'd like
To be able to give you
The whole book. But would you
Accept it? Could you? Can you take

This, which is offered, and neither
Long for, look for, hope for, expect
Anything else? (You understand,
I suspect, perhaps more

Than most, that there is in fact
Nothing else.) But still I would wish
That even from so little,
So nothing as this, I could contrive

Inexhaustible riches—richer, stranger
Even (if that were possible,
Which of course it is not)
Than yourself. O not just

An antidote for toothache
Or the antique hip, nor yet
An opposite that is equal to
The anger of sleepless nights, the fear

Of flying that is different from but like
The fear of falling—depth
As terrible as height—or of the dark
That is always growing longer

And farther from the light. I wish
I had something better than this
To give you. I know that you
Do not, cannot, always believe me,

And will not now. Still I feel I must
Say to you that I would even
Go so far as to give you
Myself (if it were mine to give,

Which, of course, it is not,
Nor should be). Or, much better
(Though still, of course, impossible), you
To yourself. Now that would be a thing

Worth giving, would it not? Together
With the pale locked green
Of that departed summer
And the bitter black box

You can neither choose nor refuse
Another, tied with a rose-colored ribbon,
That would be yours
And yours only, brimming with light.

A REUNION

for J. and M.B.

I'm sorry, my dears,
    That in each other's presence,
After so many and such
    Curious years, we should feel—
Even if not only
    (Surely, not only?)—
More alien
    Than a giraffe. I acknowledge,
Alas, the condition, which,
    Hopefully, please
Somebody, please heaven, none
    Of us actually noticed. I'm afraid
That also, in fact, there is
    Precious little
Any of us can do about it.
    But this is my fault, not yours—
The odd gait, the long
    Neck and even longer legs,
The suggestion
    Of spiders, fragile
As glasses or spindles—these
    Nervous preoccupations and
Torturous inner windings
    Are mine, not yours. As is
This altogether bizarre
    Proliferation of brown
And white spots, not to mention
    The awkward, amiable amble
Away from the truth
    Perhaps, but maybe
Towards the right leaf.

NOCTURNE

One night, these dreams, as black
As horses, will surely
Overwhelm us—the terminal
Troops, parading superbly
To the sound of the bells
Splitting the sides
Of the churches, the lost
Silver speech
Of the trumpets, the last
Vestige of all that we have had
So securely between us
Indiscriminately
Stripped, crashing in cymbals
All around us—
What shall we say then
To those we have left
Disarmed, defenseless, behind us?

A NEW YORK POEM

In spite of the civilized talk,
The informed and affable chatter
Echoing the excellent taste
Of walls built entirely of books,

The latest news, the best
Grammar, brown silk on the sofa,
Mozart with only one flute,
Stockhausen without any,

Something got lost between
The exquisite silverpoint sketch
And the fragile, expensive clatter
Of Baccarat and bone china—

Somewhere between and lost
In these comfortable, urbane rooms
The windows where anyone trying
Can see, without looking, quite clearly

The man toppling down, and dying.
But this is not good news.
We don't like it. We refuse
These sudden, uncomfortable views.

FIVE

AFTER THE LAO

I

These are my countries
My forests
And fields full of fires:
In the tiger's gold eye
A world and an occasion: love
In my crazy house on stilts
And my latitude of gold
Inhabited by a race of dancers
Whose slightest posturing
Is itself both end and beginning
As, from the end of innocence,
They contrive an eloquence
Ambiguous as leaves.

Om . . .
Like a white tree
In you I will find my talisman
    Om, Sathātheti!
You are like a ghost in my house
    Om . . .
I will know the intricacy of your silence
I will be acquainted with your grief
I will reside forever in your nations
    Om, Maha saming!
In you I will become my enemies.

III

Came then into the forest
And up into horizon
Over the edge of the world
And into the heart's country
One long month's journey
Crossed mountains and down into jungle
In that imperturbable weather
On deep road in huge green
Where were no villages
Among those silences
But heart's country was populous
The mountains were people
Wore hats contrived of vines
In caves the wind had a hundred voices
One long year's journey
Swam up into cities of cloud
Our language was the language of birds
Whistling with wings.

The journey was inside us
Sun bore down and overcame us
With jackfruit, mangoes and citrons
Until we moved on
And deeper than down is
The road unwound like silk before us
Entangled in spiders' webs
Lost in strange scents
Shaken by every little wind.

Came then into that secret place
We did not know of
Where a hundred birds sang

On every branch on every leaf
Firetrees, peacocks and herons
Everywhere there were flowers
The journey was forgotten
A wasp was heard, its glass wings
Whirring in search of the pollen.

IV

    Divinities
Who are the populace of trees
Who inhabit the smoke on the mountains
Who live in deep caves
Who swim beautifully in our rivers
    Indra, Yama
    Lokápala, the four spirits of the world
    Angels and archangels
In our fastnesses we pray
That we may bear witness
Always in our own language.

O banyan with beautiful leaves
A bird will make his house
In your shadow.

What do you say?
Perhaps it will be a starling
The color of a mackerel . . .

Will you make room for him
In the windy world of your branches?
Or are you afraid
That he will eat your fruit?

He will be eating his own heart
And will not disturb
Your vegetable silence.

If you touch him with your fingers
You will be touching yourself.

Like yours, my heart
Is most difficult of access
And desperately repels me.

VI

Body, you have lost your lodger
Now you are less than nothing
Windows blind, rooms empty
Now you can only be
A useless thing of this earth only
Like the trunk of a dead tree.

Lodger, you have left your body
Now for a time you are free
Heart-whole, eyes wide open
Now for a time you can see
Yourself unadorned and in glory
Like the green heart of a tree.

Come swiftly, soul
By forgotten footpath
And unswept track
Out of trackless
Wild or salt waste
Return to us.

Do not delay on the road
Nor hesitate overlong
In the cobra's nest
Or the tiger's thicket.

Do not let riverflood
Dissuade you nor
Any other voice
Persuade you but

Come swiftly back
To these well-wrought
Timbers, hooked eaves
Open eyes and mouth
Of your own house.

VIII

Sakké, Kamé
Twin climbers of the paradise stair
From whom light springs
Even in the midst of darkness
Charoupé, Attārikhé
Cloud-sailors, sky-walkers
Who through our midnights float
As swimmers in clear air
Khirisi Indweller
In whom we have our home
You, and also you
Who are still nameless
Gods of mountain, field and river
We pray you look not ill
On us who stumble to your altars
But lend your ears to our beseeching.

This is my world and weather
Countries of my ruined house
Locked in their fastnesses
Their colors fading on my sleeve
All this landscape gone to seed
Cities of stone, cities
Of sandalwood returned
Each year to their own dust
Under the immemorial fading fall
Of constant suns, of constant snows—

Alas! I am not what I was
Am more foreign now
For being loved. But O
If I could only wear
The singing countries of my heart
Once more upon my sleeve.

SIX

TIGER-BALM GARDENS

Tiger, the balm exceeds
All propriety, hiding your crimes
From almond eyes, leaf eyes
That would probe your commerce
Deep to its gigantic root.

Climbing to the White Pagoda,
Winding through the phony cliffs
And the strange hell of beasts,
The madonnas with blank eyes
Winking from their shadowy niches,

Mr. Yeung said, "I know you,
Tiger," and smiled when the
Horned mice ran up the walls.
"And I knew your dead father,
Who foundered his own ship

Full of men and money
Off the smoky Paracels, to
'Escape any fond detection,'
His brother your uncle being
Magistrate. Afterwards, among

The empty coffins and the white
Funerals, crying, hinting
Of great loss, of outrage,
In his house under the cliff,
Counterfeited with the same

Men and drowned money . . ."
For each separate crime

A plaster animal—as, catalogue:
A tiger, winged, under
Two coiling Chinese dragons,

A mantis bigger than a man,
A stag giving birth to a toad,
A whale, five fantastic fishes,
An elephant, and a pot-bellied
Yellow saint counting his money . . .

Exceeds, exceeds all propriety:
The medicine man, magician,
Mandarin with spotted coat
Padding over the tiles to the pool,
The jade fish eating his money,

The madonnas with blank eyes
Watching from the shadows
As we climb the stair,
Past the house built specially
For the old man's ashes,

And up to the White Pagoda,
Where Mr. Yeung said, "And for
What? You are not hidden,
Tiger," and smiled as the
Horned mice ran up the walls.

TWO POEMS AFTER THE INDONESIAN OF CHAIRIL ANWAR

ABOUT MYSELF

When my time's up
I don't want to listen
To anyone's tears—no
Not even yours
I'm sick of all this crying.

So here I am
After God knows how many years
Still untamed
Alone in my own skin
The same as any other
Beast prowling the jungle.

What can the guns say
To change that? Do you think
The bullets' idiot tattoo
Will say anything remotely new?

One just goes on
From one wound to another
From the first little pain
To its big brother
Until it's time to lie down
Until it's time to quit.

When my time's up
I won't care anymore. But not
Yet, please, not yet—
I want to live at least
Another thousand years.

II
VOICES

For those of us who lie
Between Krawang and Bekasi
Never again will there be
Any shouts of
Freedom! Merdéka!
Before taking aim again.
For us, it is finished.

    But if we return in the small hours
    Between midnight and morning
    Surely someone will hear us?
    Surely someone will listen
    To his heart's-blood coursing
    And hear, not his own,
    But our hearts still beating?

We will speak to you in the small hours
Between midnight and morning
When the clock talks to itself on the wall
And you lie awake listening
And listening to the silence
Thinking about nothing.

    We were very lucky.
    We died young.
    We left nothing
    But dust, dust
    And scattered bones.
    We were very lucky.
    For us, it is finished.

And yet, it is not finished.
It is never finished.
If you wish to remember us, remember

    We gave what we could afford
    And it was not enough.
    We gave all that we had
    And it was not enough.
    And then we gave ourselves
    And others, many others
    Into death's safekeeping
    And still it was not enough.

Even as we lie here
Hundreds, thousands, millions
Still walk about
Going nowhere
Thinking about nothing
Listening to the silence and hearing
The empty echo where the heart was.

    We were lucky.
    We died young.
    We left nothing
    But dust, dust
    And scattered bones.

And now even these
Do not belong to us.
The bones are yours now.
You will have to decide
What to do with them.
You will have to decide

Whether we died
For freedom, victory and the future
Or for nothing.
We do not know.
We cannot tell you.
The dust has got our tongues.
You will have to speak for us.

We were the lucky ones.
We died young.
We left nothing
But dust, dust
And scattered bones
All the way from
Krawang to Bekasi.

THE BONEPICKERS

for M.B.

In the jungle, growing steadily
Greener, as always, drinking
Its fill of light at the teeming
Core of the emerald, the inexhaustible
Jewel-heart: from that first step
Ashore, and that never-seen-before,
Long-looked-forward-to, half-
Remembered estuary: the gulls
Hurling their white warnings
Smoke rising from the cooking fires
Papa Portugee licking his fingers
Mama plucking her snow-white hens
And laughing at them
As though they were children:

Then down the dying path
Still bleeding with orchids
Into the enormous, incomprehensible
Green of the river basin: one
By one nails peeling skin
Shedding hair falling mind
Reeling: the world reduced to one
Bird suddenly, inexplicably
Ablaze, scattering
Diamonds in dead water:

All the roots of all the trees
Perpetually drinking
And the river outdrinking them all:
Salt from skin, good blood
From iron, chalk from bones
And the bones go on stumbling:

73

Under the roof-sized leaves
Through the heart of a tree
And into the clearing
To find what everyone comes for:

Papa Portugee perched on a skull
Mama with her one
Thumbnail curved like a needle
And all around them the children:
Holes for eyes and hair rotting
Their mouths full of iron
Delicately picking and pulling
Until, like all the others before you,
Headbone heartbone heelbone
You're finally clean, and shining.

THE GOAT

Comes to us crooked from his Greek wood,
His beard thorn-ridden, quick with fleas,
A hunchback, riddled with disease,
But standing where he's always stood,

Eyeing the same wood-nymphs and sad
Ladies. Coughs, then munches his cans.
Steps gingerly, as though he's glad
He can step at all, whose savage dance

Was all the ladies needed once
To turn them silk and daft as leaves.
Apples, melons, and yellow quince:
He blinks an eye awry and grieves

That last departed feast: the food
Fit only for an important god.
Paws fitfully at the dry sod
Under the old trees, who once was good

As god, and made the wood-nymphs glad
To be alive and green as the trees
He killed them in. A little mad
Now, his wits addled by a strange unease,

He wanders off to the edge of the wood
Where nymph and lady, passing, wince,
And avert their eyes as ladies should;
And sniff sachets, and shake their fans.

And wonder, meantime, why their hands
Should sprout new leaves and break into bud,
Then suddenly curve into claws instead
As in their helpless, headlong dance

They wheel in a circle, as schoolgirls would,
Around and around his severed head.

THREE BIRDS

I
PEACOCK

All eyes, he looks oddly askance
At all the world, and nothing sees
(For all his hundred eyes' remove)
But his own arch magnificence:
Who walks, contained, aloof, in love
A hundred times into himself,
Discovering in the mirror's trance
Interior geographies
Of topaz, amethyst and quartz,
Communicating in his dance
A bird more beautiful than himself,
Until by love he learns at last
His station and most proper stance:
The mannered pose, the poise that is
Impeccably correct and strange,
The downward, secret, oblique glance,
The stately motions of disdain
That nothing sees nor cares nor knows
Of ordinary tame substance,
As backward through the mirror goes
That other bird (whose tail's a harp
The wind has tuned to opulence,
Whose metal, precious eye's a map
Of every lonely, secret place)
Towards that intolerable silence
At mirror heart. There, all eyes again,
He turns (almost, begins to sing)
Back to the world of Innocents,
Who nothing know of what he knows
In their wildest imagining:
Who knows, at last, true elegance.

PHOENIX

From his sad nest of bonfires
Looks blindly out, while all our instruments
Record his marriage, plunging their live wires
Deeper than scandals to convince
Us he's the origin of fires.
Unused to eloquence,

This bird, long since convicted of
Volcanoes, protests his innocence again,
And Everest crumbles. When he tries to prove
He's harmless, earthquakes begin.
The whole air burns when he's in love.
The mountain's heart's a ruin.

His gait is clockwork, printing fire
And fusing rock (in which live fossils writhe)
Under his delicate step, until desire
Snaps his head up like a scythe,
And all our proud engines misfire.
In love he's long, and lithe

As flames, never more beautiful
Than now, when on his incandescent nest
He hatches all the world from its stone shell,
And then slips under Everest
To sleep a thousand years, until
His myth's made manifest.

III
HAWK

Chuckle-eyed, the looping hawk
Catches pigeons in his talk,

Dispatches centuries of birds
In the flash and tumble of his words,

In the holy crack of his wings,
Where he makes a church, and sings

Murder like a choir. He knows
That what he is, death does,

And dazzling, drops him like a stone
To swoop, slash, and seize again,

Making sermons as he gnaws
His own hawk's heart in his claws.

Wedded to himself, as knitted
Flesh ripples sleek hide
And slides with the good
Blood towards bone: It's me!
I'm mine!—the loud
Cry looks like cloud in a
Cartoon, as the sparks fly
From his hooves, ignite
His dazzling thatch,
And in succeeding frames
Torch both farmer's roof
And sybil's leaves: I cry?
Who cares?—tosses
His blazing mane and cuts
His own fantastic shape
Through walls or doors or trees:
Look now! I'm here!—then
Disappears, as the plough-
Horse flips the plough
And kills the corn.
                Pursued
By farmer and by nymph,
Each in love with the other
Half, he gallops on,
Ignoring both, disdaining
Reins, spurring himself
With whips of thorns: You love?
Me too!—himself above
Himself below, the blood
That bubbles up to brain
Pours down as well:
Through wrist and elbow,

Withers and hoof, to
Celebrate his marriage to
The only love of his life—
That never can be other than
The other half of himself.

EPILOGUE FOR A BESTIARY

And then departed: all the Ark
Returned to the original dark:
Zebra, peacock, horse and shark,
    Following their shadows.

The child asleep watches them go:
Lion, elephant and doe:
Going farther than they know,
    Following their shadows.

Under the bitter, bleeding trees:
Goat and centaur and their fleas.
As deadroot follows stone, so these,
    Following their shadows.

How shall they go? Without a word?
Insect, animal and bird
All gone, and no one even heard?
    Following their shadows,

In silence, as they came. No talk
Can halt that final, fatal walk:
Phoenix, tiger, ibex, hawk,
    Following their shadows.

Within the space it takes to make
Only one dream and then awake,
All gone, all gone, giraffe and snake,
    Following their shadows?

Hoof and paw and tooth and horn
As though they never had been born:
Leopard, bull and unicorn,
    Following their shadows.

All gone? But look—the child—beware!
Is dancing with his dancing bear,
And soon we'll all be dancing there,
    Following our shadows.

LISTENING TO DOGS

(apologies to Auden)

This one won't talk, but he will
Shout, at the drop
Of a hat that
Nobody wears anymore—

As, at the ignored because
Imperceptible step
Of a lady he loved dearly, who
Died three years ago, he

Shouts at the garbage-men
An hour before they're due,
At the gardeners
After they're gone, and

Most clearly, un-
Mistakably, very loudly,
Shouts, probably a curse
In the guise of a warning, but maybe

A greeting, to the sweet
Brutal kids stumbling
Out of school to plague him
Every day at three o'clock.

* * *

But this one is a true
Talker. He babbles on, a whole
Tower of Babel, at the drop
Of the same hat. His shout

(Alas, he does that also)
Is a kind of odd, perturbable
Grumble. He also
Loves the lady, in fact has known her

Longer than anyone, knows
All about the kids
Looking for sweets, for suitable cans
To tie a tail to, has made

Friends, and enemies, of
Garbage-men and gardeners. But
He talks. What
Does he say? I'd like

To be able to tell you. But
I can't. I've no idea. I only know it's
Talk—if expressed
Without verbs, in nouns only.

IN MEMORY OF ISAK DINESEN

Returned now we can only hope
To Africa and the morning
She loved especially for its light
As the liquid sun
Swam up from the plains
And onto her porches
Before rising higher in the lion's eyes
And the eyes of the hunters
Walking out between the columns
And up to the edge of the sky
(Their guns riding high on their shoulders)
To look down from the young
Hills towards the valley as it shed
Its leaves
And filled with air.

Returned if she is dealt with fairly
To her house the size of her heart
And the dark young voices
She loved especially for what they could not say
As the broken sentences
Faltered up the stair
And down the corridor
To fumble, like the light, at her door
(Which she always opened)
Demanding, loving, knowing
Her love was in the thick of living
Shaping with their hands as much as hers
Animals and farms and stories
Out of the morning
Light and the young hills.

SCROLLPAINTING

Hard as anyone's hands, soft as their least touch,
The landscape behind this hand-high delicate beast
Grows slowly out of the silence. Beyond,
Black iron and moss where the hills ride up;
Nearer, pale sun and paler moon
Together trapped in twigs in the snowy woods
As the mandarin's scroll continues to unroll,
Shedding its dead or still dying pages. Cleftfoot
Warily poised at the very edge of the wood,
Suspicious of so much softness: anyone can tell
He is but newly come down from the mountain.
If he stays, he will learn. Here, spring
Will be sudden, and the thunder announcing rain
Will speak with a new voice, not the iron
Bellnote he remembers. If he stays, he will learn
To read the grave's green histories in the back-
Broken sad palms of the palms and palmetto
Shoots as they spring out of the tame fields
And frozen paddies, so that his horns also,
As tortured as a tree, push up with the vines
Ruddy with sunstroke; break
Into leaf; blossom. But look where now the fine
Neck arches and the light leaps under the iron
Branches as the scroll unrolls to the end
And he stands still, with his head
High, and listens. Listen. It is not a voice
Many would care to remember, but for him
It's halfway home. It is the voice of the wind
Off the mountain, from which he is so newly
Come down—but for one hour only,
And impelled by but the one desire: to leave
Hoofprints in the blazing snow outside

For the mandarin to marvel at when he
Rolls up his scroll at last and walks stiffly
Out of his house, into the world, in the morning.

RONALD PERRY was born in 1932 in Miami, Florida. After receiving an M.A. in English literature and history from the University of Miami in 1954, he spent two years in the Army as a cryptographer before accepting a creative writing fellowship at the State University of Iowa, which he abandoned when he decided he did not want to teach. Since then he has worked as an airline reservations agent in Miami, as secretary to an American engineering firm in Vientiane, Laos, and as an advertising and public relations executive in Nassau, Bahamas, where he still lives. From 1954, when his poems were first published, until 1970, his work appeared fairly regularly in magazines. During the same period, he also published four books of poetry—*The Fire Nursery and Other Poems* (1956), *The Rock Harbor* (1959), *The Pipe Smokers* (1960), and *Voyages from Troy* (1962). After a ten-year silence, he returns to publication with this volume, which includes a number of poems written in the last two years.